FEB 2 1 2005

DUE

The Kids' Career Library™

A Day in the Life of a
Firefighter

Mary Bowman-Kruhm
and Claudine G. Wirths

The Rosen Publishing Group's
PowerKids Press™
New York

Thanks to Jennifer Morimoto, David Swanson, and the Montgomery County, Maryland, Fire Department.

Published in 1997, 2003 by The Rosen Publishing Group, Inc.
29 East 21st Street, New York, NY 10010

Revised Edition 2003

Editor: Jannell Khu

Text Revisions: Jennifer Way

Book Design: Erin McKenna

Photo Illustrations: All photo illustrations by Kelly Hahn.

Bowman-Kruhm, Mary.
    A day in the life of a firefighter / by Mary Bowman-Kruhm and Claudine G. Wirths.
        p.   cm. — (The kids' career library)
    Includes index.
    Summary: Describes the daily responsibilities, tasks, and life of a firefighter.
    ISBN 0-8239-6809-X
    1. Fire extinction—Juvenile literature. [1. Fire extinction. 2. Firefighters. 3. Occupations.] I. Wirths, Claudine G. II. Title. III. Series.
    TH9148.B68 1997
    628.9'25—dc21

                                     96-53129

Manufactured in the United States of America

Contents

1   A Firefighter's Day Starts   5

2   Ready to Go   6

3   Training   9

4   Help!   10

5   Lights and Sirens   13

6   At the Fire   14

7   Writing a Report   17

8   Schoolchildren Visit   18

9   Helpful Hoses   21

10   Home at Last?   22

   Glossary   23

   Index   24

   Web Sites   24

A Firefighter's Day Starts

Firefighter Jennifer Morimoto arrives at the station by 7:00 A.M. and leaves at 5:00 P.M. The night crew is still on duty when Firefighter Morimoto gets to the station. The night crew leaves when the day crew arrives. There are always firefighters at the station in case there is a fire somewhere. Firefighter Morimoto takes off her coat. Then she carefully puts her firefighter gear near the fire truck. She is now ready if the station gets a fire alarm call.

◀ Firefighter Morimoto starts her day by collecting her firefighter gear.

Ready to Go

Next Firefighter Morimoto checks that the fire trucks are filled with **fuel**. She wants to be sure that they are ready to go when the fire alarm rings.

Then Firefighter Morimoto exercises. She must be strong to use the **equipment** that puts out fires. She also must be strong enough to help people out of a burning building. She **stretches**, runs, and lifts weights to stay in shape. When she finishes her exercises, Firefighter Morimoto puts on her blue uniform. She wears it underneath her firefighter gear.

Exercise helps Firefighter Morimoto stay strong for her job. ▶

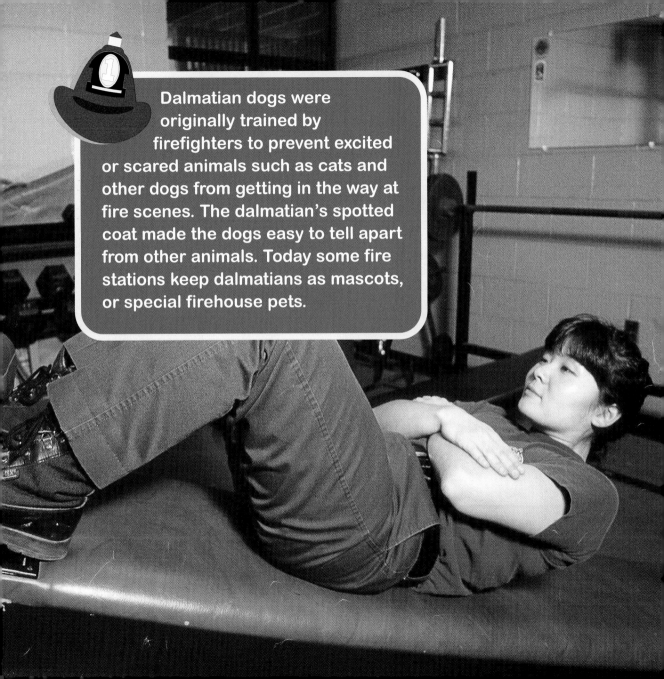

Dalmatian dogs were originally trained by firefighters to prevent excited or scared animals such as cats and other dogs from getting in the way at fire scenes. The dalmatian's spotted coat made the dogs easy to tell apart from other animals. Today some fire stations keep dalmatians as mascots, or special firehouse pets.

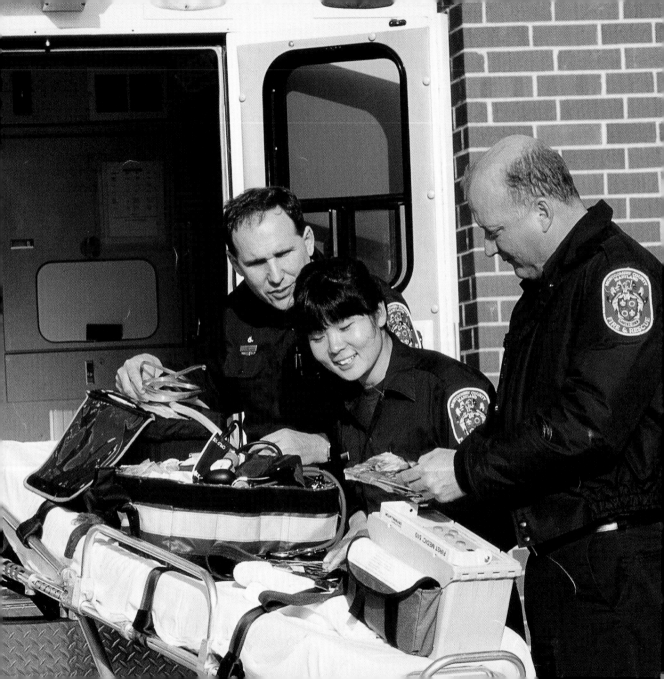

Training

Every morning, if there is no fire alarm, Firefighter Morimoto takes part in training. Training helps her to do her job better. This morning she and the rest of the firefighters learn about a new **ambulance**. They are firefighters first. However, firefighters also must know how to treat a person who has been hurt in a fire until they can get the person to a hospital. Firefighter Morimoto climbs inside the ambulance to learn how the controls, such as the **siren**, work. She also checks the medical **supplies.**

◀ Training is an important part of being a good firefighter.

9

Help!

Suddenly the fire alarm rings in the station. A person has called to report that a house is on fire. The firefighters must get there fast to put out the fire.

Firefighter Morimoto runs to get her boots, pants, jacket, and **helmet**. All of her gear is in an **organized** pile so she can put it on quickly. She grabs a gas mask, too. If she has to go into an area with heavy smoke, the mask will help her to breathe.

10

As soon as the fire alarm rings, firefighters need to get ready to go to the fire scene as soon as possible. Firefighter ▶ Morimoto is always ready to go if there is a fire.

May 4 is International Firefighters' Day. This day honors firefighters who have been hurt or who have died in the line of duty. On this day people thank firefighters for saving lives.

Lights and Sirens

Firefighter Morimoto turns on the engine of the fire truck. She turns on the lights and the siren. Two more firefighters jump on the truck.

The truck leaves the station and heads for the fire. AH-WHOO! AH-WHOO! The siren tells people that the fire truck is coming. As it roars down the street, cars move to let it pass. Many boys and girls who are walking along the street stop to watch. They wish they could ride on the fire truck.

◄ The fire truck has bright lights and loud sirens to warn cars and people to move out of the way.

At the Fire

When the firefighters get to the house, there is no fire. It was a false alarm.

"It's sad that some people think a false alarm is funny," Firefighter Morimoto says. "If there had been a real fire somewhere else, the people in that fire might have been hurt because we had gone to the false alarm." This is why calling in a false alarm is illegal.

Firefighters must answer all fire alarm calls, even if one turns out to be a false alarm. ▶

Writing a Report

Back at the station, Firefighter Morimoto writes a report on where the truck went and what the firefighters saw and did. She writes a report every time the fire truck goes out. Her report helps the firefighters to learn more about putting out fires. This time it may also help the police to catch the person who called in the false alarm. When Firefighter Morimoto finishes, she helps the other firefighters to wash the truck. Firefighters are proud of their trucks and keep them shiny and clean.

◀ Firefighter Morimoto keeps track of the alarm calls by writing reports.

17

Schoolchildren Visit

That afternoon, a class visits from a nearby school. Firefighter Morimoto tells the children what to do if their clothes catch on fire. She shows them a special fire safety rule called Stop, drop, and roll.

"Remember—
- STOP where you are,
- DROP to the ground, and
- ROLL around to put out the fire.

This rule could one day save your life," Firefighter Morimoto tells them.

Stop, drop, and roll is an important fire safety rule that everyone should know. ▶

Fire Prevention Week is the week of October 9. During this week, firefighters often visit schools to teach children about safety and preventing fires. They talk to kids about what it is like to be a firefighter.

Helpful Hoses

Later, Firefighter Morimoto and another firefighter work to fold and put away a new hose. Pulling a heavy hose is hard, so they help each other. They will help each other with the hose during a fire, too.

Water from hoses puts out a fire, but hoses help firefighters in another way. Even on a sunny day, a house can be dark as night inside because of smoke. The firefighters cannot always see through the smoke, so they follow the hose to find their way out of a dark, burning house.

◄ More than one person is needed to carry a heavy fire hose.

Home at Last?

At 5:00 P.M., Firefighter Morimoto's workday is finished. She looks for her coat and starts to get ready to leave.

Suddenly the bell in the station rings again. It is another fire alarm! Once again she grabs her gear and runs to the fire truck. The night crew has not yet come to work, so the day crew must do the job. Firefighter Morimoto does not complain. "We are firefighters. We go to the fire no matter what time it is," she says proudly.

AH-WHOO! Away she goes again!

Glossary

ambulance (AM-byoo-lens) A special truck for carrying people who are sick or hurt to the hospital.

equipment (uh-KWIP-mint) All the supplies needed to do an activity.

fuel (FYOOL) Something that is used to make energy, warmth, or power.

helmet (HEL-mit) A covering worn to keep the head safe.

organized (OR-guh-nyzd) Neat and in order.

siren (SY-ren) An instrument that makes a loud sound.

stretches (STREH-chez) Bends and reaches out to loosen muscles and to stay in good shape.

supplies (suh-PLYZ) Things a person needs to do a job.

Index

A
ambulance, 9

C
crew, 5, 22

E
exercises, 6

F
false alarm,
    14, 17

fire alarm, 6,
    9–10, 22
fire truck(s),
    5–6, 13,
    17, 22
fuel, 6

G
gas mask, 10
gear, 5–6,
    10, 22

H
helmet, 10
hose, 21

R
report, 17

S
siren, 9, 13
station, 5, 10,
    13, 17,
    22

supplies, 9

T
training, 9

U
uniform, 6

W
weights, 6

Web Sites

Due to the changing nature of Internet links, PowerKids Press has developed an online list of Web sites related to the subject of this book. This site is updated regularly. Please use this link to access the list:
www.powerkidslinks.com/kcl/dlfire/

24